THE NAME OF YAHWEH, ANGELS AND THE GARDEN OF MY HEART

Written by
Lindi Masters

Illustrated by
Lizzie Masters

Published by

Seraph Creative

Heaven's Heart for Earth

Written by©
Lindi Masters

Illustrated and Designed© by
Lizzie Masters

Special thanks to IGNITE KIDZHUB© for their contributions to the story.

Acknowledgment and thanks to Ian Clayton and Son of Thunder Publications© for reference.

This edition published by
SERAPH CREATIVE in 2018

All rights reserved. No part of this publication may be reproduced, stored in a retrieval system or transmitted, in any form or by any means, electronic, mechanical, photocopying, recording or otherwise, without the prior permission of the copyright holder.

ISBN 978-0-9946974-7-9

CONTENTS

10 Layers of Angels 4-10

The Garden of my Heart 11-14

The Name of Yahweh 15-19

Art by KIDZHUB 20- 24

10 LAYERS OF ANGELS

Angels are created by God and are sent to help us.

They bring us messages and they watch over us.

They protect us and they even come to talk to us.

Angels like to laugh and are very funny.

They love to worship and love to sing,

'HOLY HOLY HOLY!'

But not all Angels are the same.

There are different Angels and there are millions of them.

They get their names from what jobs they do.

And not all Angels have wings!

They love to talk about Yahweh.

When we talk about Yahweh they get **EXCITED!**

Let's name some of the Angels...

Chayos are...

The holy living creatures.
Their boss is Metatron.
And he is the key maker of all the doors in heaven.

Ophenim are...

The wheels inside wheels.
Like a ball inside a ball.
Their boss is Raziel.

Erelim are...

The mighty ones.
The Angels that get stuff done.
Their chief is Tzathkiel.

Kashmelian are...

The brilliant and shining ones.
They change colour like a chameleon.

They like to be funny.
Their chief is Tzadkiel.

Seraphim are... The burning ones.

They have six wings and their job is to get us ready to do stuff. Their chief is Gabriel.

Malachim are... The Kings.

They bring Yahweh's judgement to the earth. Their chief is Uriel.

Elohym are...
Angels that look like us.
They look like humans.
Their chief is Haniel.

Ben Ei Elohym are...

The Sons of God that God first created.
They sit on the thrones and wait
for us to take over.
Their chief is Michael.

Cherubim are...

The covering ones. They have four faces. The lion, the ox, the eagle and the man.
Their chief is Raphael.

Ishim are...

The prince warrior angels.

They fight for our destiny and guard the glory in our lives.
Their chief is Sandelford.

The Garden of my Heart

I can build a garden in my heart.

This is a safe and special place with God.

A place to know Jesus loves me and we are friends there.

The blood of Jesus opens the door.

I close my eyes and step into the river of God through the door of my imagination.

The river of God flows into my garden.

I start walking into the river.

This river is full of gold, diamonds, stones and beauty.

The leaves on the trees are living beings that move in the water like fish.

I walk up the river to the presence of The Father.

I walk down the path to the bridge.

In my garden I find flowers and trees.

Sometimes animals.

I can plant things in my garden.

And I can come back again and Jesus will never get bored.

This is my happy place.

The Name of Yahweh
YHVH
YOD-HEY-VAV-HEY

It is one of the names of God used in Hebrew.

It can also be written as **HVHY** like the Jewish people write it.

In Hebrew we write it like this and read it from right to left.

יהוה

Reading it from right to left.

יהוה

HEY   VAV   HEY   YOD

When we sing and use the name

יהוה YHVH

we go into each letter.

Hebrew letters are living beings and are alive.

YHVH יהוה means 'I am' or 'To be'.

YHVH יהוה is very old and very holy.

Let's say a prayer.

Close your eyes.

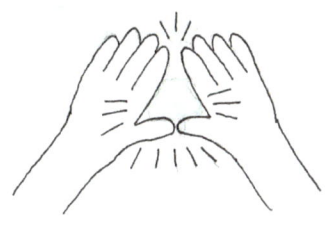 Make a triangle with your hands.

Sing the Name of **YHVH** יהוה through the triangle.

Sing it like this

 Step into the Name of

יהוה **YHVH**

and through the veil.

Step into the river flowing from God's throne.

Stop and look at the angels around you.

Tell them that you are happy to see them and are happy that they are with you.

Now you can step into the garden of your heart and play and talk with Jesus.

When you are ready, you can step back through the veil and the name of YHVH יהוה.

Erelim Angel (top left) - Hendriette, 11

Angels in the Garden of my Heart (top right) - Reuben, 9

Angel (bottom left) and Ishim Angels (bottom right) - Judah, 6

Angels around the Throne (top right) - Reuben, 9

Guardian Angel - Reuben, 9

Kashmelian Angels (middle right) and Uriel (bottom right) - Hendriette, 11

Garden of my Heart (top right)
- Judah, 6

**Angels around the Throne (top left)
and My Happy Place (bottom right)**
- Reuben, 9

Breaking of Bread (top left) - Anna

Haniel (top right) - Hendriette, 11

Warrior Angels in the garden (bottom right) - Jeiel, 7

Warring Angels (bottom left) - Reuel, 4

**Personal Angels
(top left) - Jeiel, 7**

**Warring Angels
(top right) -
Reuel, 4**

**Ishim Angels
(bottom left) -
Hendriette, 11**

**Realms of
Kingdom
(bottom right) -
Judah, 6**

www.ingramcontent.com/pod-product-compliance
Lightning Source LLC
Chambersburg PA
CBHW041438010526
44118CB00002B/118